Eels

Tori Miller

PowerKiDS
press

New York

Published in 2009 by The Rosen Publishing Group, Inc.
29 East 21st Street, New York, NY 10010

First Edition

Editor: Joanne Randolph
Book Design: Greg Tucker
Photo Researcher: Jessica Gerweck

Photo Credits: Cover, pp. 5, 11, 12–13, 19 Shutterstock.com; p. 7 © Paul Sutherland/Getty Images; p. 9 © Stephen Frink/Getty Images; pp. 15, 21 © Norbert Wu/Getty Images; p. 17 © Tim Laman/Getty Images.

Library of Congress Cataloging-in-Publication Data

Miller, Tori.
  Eels / Tori Miller. — 1st ed.
      p. cm. — (Freaky fish)
  Includes index.
  ISBN 978-1-4358-2754-7 (library binding) — ISBN 978-1-4358-3170-4 (pbk.)
ISBN 978-1-4358-3176-6 (6-pack)
  1. Eels—Juvenile literature. I. Title.
  QL637.9.A5M55 2009
  597'.43—dc22
                                    2008030456

Manufactured in the United States of America

Contents

Eel Surprise!

A little fish is swimming in a **shallow** bay. Suddenly, a large snakelike animal darts out from behind a rock. It is an eel! The fish swims away fast, but the eel is faster. The eel catches the fish with its sharp teeth. The fish cannot get away. The eel eats the fish quickly and then goes back to its hiding place to wait for more **prey**.

Even though eels are fish, they have a long, thin body that makes them look like underwater snakes. People have been interested in eels for many years. Scientists, or people who study the world, are working to learn more about them.

Here you can see this moray eel's teeth in the front of its mouth. It also has another set of teeth in its throat that it pushes up into its mouth to pull prey into its throat!

So Many Eels

Eels have been around for over 93 million years. There are many different kinds of eels. In fact, there are more than 500 kinds!

The skin of an eel is thick and **slimy**. Some eels have small scales. Other eels have no scales. Scales are the small plates of skin that cover some animals' bodies.

Eels can be found in many different colors. Many eels are black or brown. Eels can also be red, yellow, green, or blue. Some eels have spots or other markings on them. Baby eels do not have any color at all. They are see-through!

This is a sharp-tailed snake eel. Unlike other eels, the snake eel has a hard tail.

Underwater Snakes

Eels are not really snakes, but they look a lot like them! Eels have long tube-shaped bodies. An eel's fins are different from most other fish's. An eel has one long fin that runs from the back of its head all the way to its tail. An eel sometimes has two small **pectoral fins** near its head. An eel swims by moving its whole body in a wave, as do snakes.

Some kinds of eels can grow very long. Conger eels can be 20 feet (6 m) long! Some eels are very small, growing to be only a few inches (cm) long. However, most eels are around 3 feet (1 m) long.

You can see the wavelike movements this ribbon eel makes as it swims. Ribbon eels generally grow to be around 3 feet (1 m) long.

Eel Homes

Eels can be found in both salt water and freshwater. They live in freshwater rivers, lakes, and ponds. There may be eels in the lakes and streams where you live! They can also be found in the Atlantic Ocean and Pacific Ocean. European and American eels live in salt water for part of their lives and then **migrate** to freshwater.

Eels like places where they can hide. They like to hide behind rocks or in **coral reefs**. Some eels bury themselves in the sand. Large **colonies** of eels can be found in some coral reefs.

You will often see eels, like this purple-mouth moray, poking their heads out of holes in coral reefs or rocks. They hide and wait for a yummy fish to swim past.

The Eel:
Freaky Facts

- Electric eels are not really eels. They are knifefish.

- Eels breathe through their skin as well as through their gills, which are body parts fish use to breathe.

- Eels can move over land for short amounts of time.

- Some kinds of eels have blood that is **poisonous** to people.

- An eel's slimy coating keeps it safe from illnesses.

- It takes European eels three years to swim from the Sargasso Sea to freshwater.

○ Eels die soon after they mate.

○ Baby eels look so different from adult eels that for a long time scientists thought they were a different kind of fish.

○ Not all eels prey on smaller animals. The snub-nosed eel digs through the skin of larger fish and then eats it from the inside out.

A Closer Look: The Moray Eel

There are about 200 different kinds of moray eels. Most morays are about 3 feet (1 m) long. Some morays are dark brown, black, or gray while others are bright blue or red. Morays do not have scales.

Morays live in the ocean. They do not hear or see well, so morays use their sense of smell to hunt. Once they smell their prey, they catch it with their sharp teeth. Morays generally keep their big mouths open to let water move through their gills.

Morays can be a danger, but only if they are **threatened**. It is not a good idea to try to make friends with a moray eel!

These white-eyed moray eels make their homes in coral reefs. Morays like to eat small fish, octopuses, squid, and even other eels.

Eel Enemies

Eels are most likely to become another animal's dinner when they are young because of their small size. As eels get bigger, the size of the animals that hunt them becomes bigger, too. Eels can be eaten by other fish, octopuses, birds, and some land animals. Eels are one of the otter's favorite foods!

Eels keep from being eaten by hiding. Sometimes they can get away if they are caught because their slimy skin makes them hard to hold onto. Eels can also use their powerful mouths and sharp teeth to protect themselves.

This puffin carries a mouthful of small eels back to its nest. Puffins live in cold waters and dive and catch many fish at one time.

What a Life!

Eels can be big, but like most other animals, they start out much smaller. Baby eels hatch, or break free, from eggs. Newly hatched eels are called **larvae**. Eel larvae are small and leaf shaped.

American eels swim to the Sargasso Sea, near Bermuda, to have babies. When the larvae hatch, they are carried on ocean currents to the United States' East Coast. On the way, the larvae turn into pinky-sized, brown **elvers**. The elvers swim up rivers into freshwater lakes and ponds. In a few months, the elvers change again, growing several feet (m) to become adult eels.

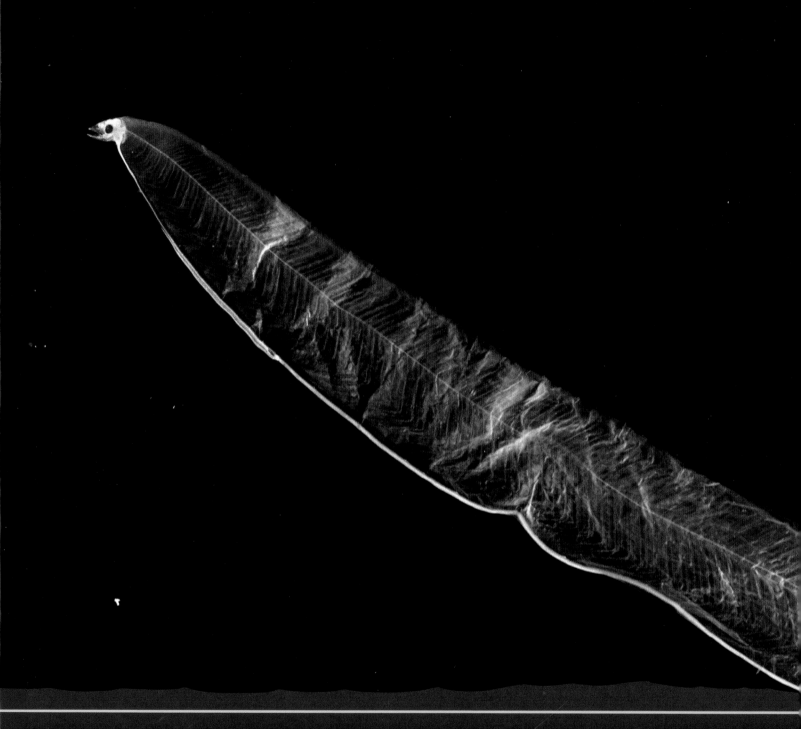

American and European eel larvae, such as this one, move from the Sargasso Sea to freshwater. They return to the Sargasso Sea when they are ready to mate.

Eels and People

People are one of the biggest enemies of eels. People have been eating eels for many years. This is especially true in Japan. Have you ever eaten eel?

Public aquariums often have eels. If you live near an aquarium, you may be able to see some for yourself! Some people keep eels in smaller home aquariums. People who keep eels as pets must care for them properly. It is not easy to keep a pet eel fed and healthy. It is fun to learn about eels, but remember, eels are happiest when they are left alone.

Glossary

attacks (uh-TAKS) Tries to hurt someone or something.

colonies (KAH-luh-neez) Groups that live together.

coral reefs (KOR-ul REEFS) Underwater hills of coral, or hard matter made up of the bones of tiny sea animals.

crustaceans (krus-TAY-shunz) Animals that have no backbones, have hard shells, and live mostly in water.

elvers (EL-verz) Young eels.

larvae (LAHR-vee) Insects or fish in the early period of life in which they have a wormlike form.

migrate (MY-grayt) To move from one place to another.

pectoral fins (PEK-tuh-rul FINZ) The fins on the side of a fish's body.

poisonous (POYZ-nus) Causing pain or death.

prey (PRAY) An animal that is hunted by another animal for food.

shallow (SHA-loh) Not deep.

slimy (SLY-mee) Thick and wet.

threatened (THREH-tund) Acted as if something could cause hurt.

Index

Web Sites

Due to the changing nature of Internet links, PowerKids Press has developed an online list of Web sites related to the subject of this book. This site is updated regularly. Please use this